**The glory of gardening:
hands in the dirt, head in
the sun, heart with nature**
Alfred Austin

GARDEN PLANNER
AND LOG BOOK

An easy helpful planner

This Gardening planner comes simple and easy to follow process

INSIDE

- Supplier Info
- Garden Layout
- Schedulers
- Seasons To-Do list
- Year At A glance
- Weather Log
- TO-DO LIST
- Sow/Transplants
- Shopping List
- Plant Log
- Garden Journal/Best picture to capture
- Pest And Diseases Treatment Log
- Blank Schedulers Pages
- Extra Weather Log
- Sketch
- Dotted Graph Pages

An easy helpful planner
to begin your garden journey

THIS PLANNER
BELONGS TO

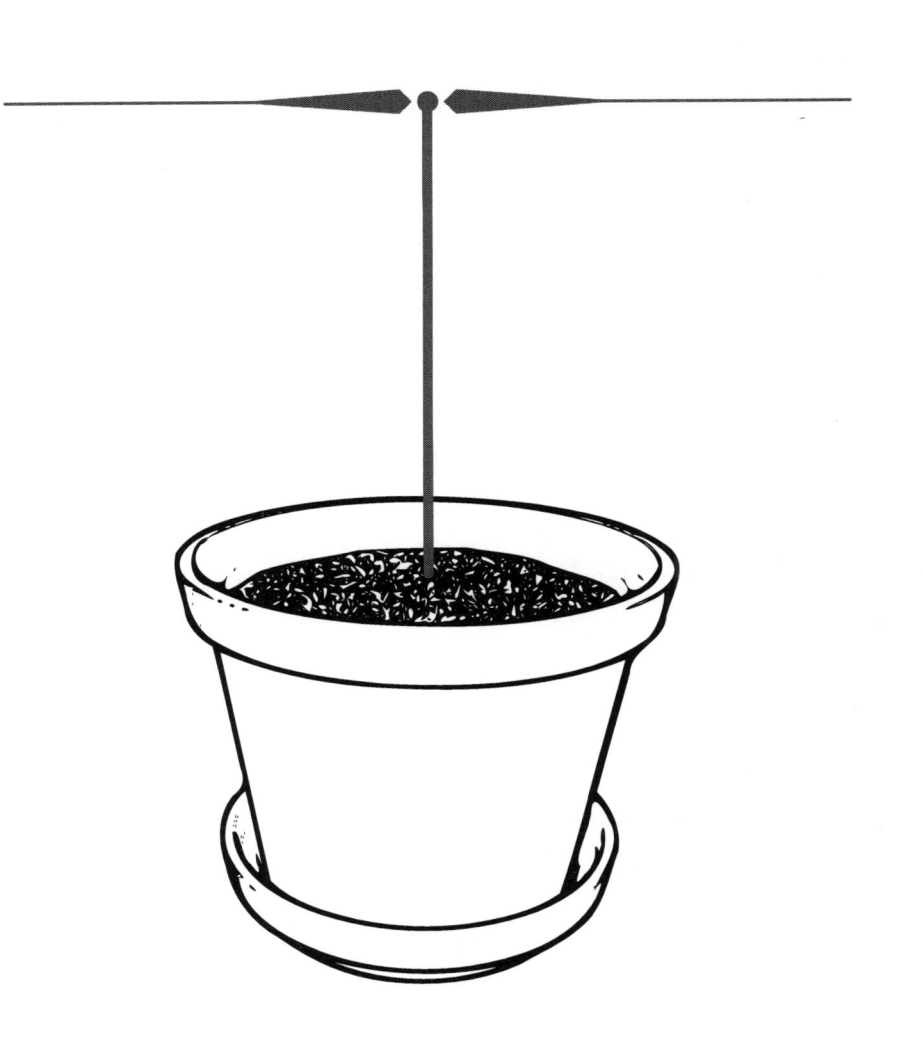

YOUR SUPPLIER INFO

Name	Shop	Location
Phone	Email	
Tele	Web	
Name	Shop	Location
Phone	Email	
Tele	Web	
Name	Shop	Location
Phone	Email	
Tele	Web	
Name	Shop	Location
Phone	Email	
Tele	Web	
Name	Shop	Location
Phone	Email	
Tele	Web	
Name	Shop	Location
Phone	Email	
Tele	Web	
Name	Shop	Location
Phone	Email	
Tele	Web	
Name	Shop	Location
Phone	Email	
Tele	Web	
Name	Shop	Location
Phone	Email	
Tele	Web	
Name	Shop	Location
Phone	Email	
Tele	Web	

YOUR SUPPLIER INFO

Name	Shop	Location
Phone	Email	
Tele	Web	

Name	Shop	Location
Phone	Email	
Tele	Web	

Name	Shop	Location
Phone	Email	
Tele	Web	

Name	Shop	Location
Phone	Email	
Tele	Web	

Name	Shop	Location
Phone	Email	
Tele	Web	

Name	Shop	Location
Phone	Email	
Tele	Web	

Name	Shop	Location
Phone	Email	
Tele	Web	

Name	Shop	Location
Phone	Email	
Tele	Web	

Name	Shop	Location
Phone	Email	
Tele	Web	

Name	Shop	Location
Phone	Email	
Tele	Web	

GARDEN LAYOUT

GARDEN LAYOUT

GARDEN LAYOUT

SCHEDULERS

Description	Jan	Feb	Mar	Apr	May	Jun	Notes

SCHEDULERS

Description	Jul	Aug	Sep	Oct	Nov	Dec	Notes

SEASONS TO DO LIST

SPRING

- ○ _____
- ○ _____
- ○ _____
- ○ _____
- ○ _____
- ○ _____
- ○ _____
- ○ _____
- ○ _____
- ○ _____

SUMMER

- ○ _____
- ○ _____
- ○ _____
- ○ _____
- ○ _____
- ○ _____
- ○ _____
- ○ _____
- ○ _____
- ○ _____

FALL

- ○ _____
- ○ _____
- ○ _____
- ○ _____
- ○ _____
- ○ _____
- ○ _____
- ○ _____
- ○ _____
- ○ _____

WINTER

- ○ _____
- ○ _____
- ○ _____
- ○ _____
- ○ _____
- ○ _____
- ○ _____
- ○ _____
- ○ _____
- ○ _____

YEAR AT A GLANCE

January	February	March

April	May	June

July	August	September

October	November	December

WEATHER LOG
33 ROWS TO LOG IN

Code	Date	Temperature	Humidity	Dew Point	Wind Speed	Wind Direction	Barometric Pressure	Rain Fall	Frost	Snow

General Observation :

Page:

January

MON	TUE	WED	THUR
☐	☐	☐	☐
☐	☐	☐	☐
☐	☐	☐	☐
☐	☐	☐	☐
☐	☐	☐	☐

FRI	SAT	SUN
☐	☐	☐
☐	☐	☐
☐	☐	☐
☐	☐	☐
☐	☐	☐

KEY DATES

PRIORITY

TO DO LIST

DATE ....

TOP 3   MON THE WED THU FRI SAT SUN

1.   2.   3.

To Do's	Priorities
★ ••••••••••••••••••••••••••••••••••	
★ ••••••••••••••••••••••••••••••••••	
★ ••••••••••••••••••••••••••••••••••	
★ ••••••••••••••••••••••••••••••••••	
★ ••••••••••••••••••••••••••••••••••	
★ ••••••••••••••••••••••••••••••••••	
★ ••••••••••••••••••••••••••••••••••	
★ ••••••••••••••••••••••••••••••••••	
★ ••••••••••••••••••••••••••••••••••	
★ ••••••••••••••••••••••••••••••••••	
★ ••••••••••••••••••••••••••••••••••	
★ ••••••••••••••••••••••••••••••••••	

NOTES

....

....

....

....

....

SOW/TRANSPLANTS

DATE ....

Sow	Transplants
★	★ ....
★	★ ....
★	★ ....
★	★ ....
★	★ ....
★	★ ....
★	★ ....
★	★ ....
★	★ ....
★	★ ....
★	★ ....
★	★ ....
★	★ ....
★	★ ....
★	★ ....
★	★ ....

NOTES

....
....
....
....

SHOPPING LIST

MON THE WED THU FRI SAT SUN

★ ....
★ ....
★ ....
★ ....
★ ....
★ ....
★ ....
★ ....
★ ....
★ ....
★ ....
★ ....
★ ....
★ ....
★ ....
★ ....
★ ....

★ ....
★ ....
★ ....
★ ....
★ ....
★ ....
★ ....
★ ....
★ ....
★ ....
★ ....
★ ....
★ ....
★ ....

NOTES

....
....
....
....

Plant Log

PLANT NAME:_____ **PURCHASE AT:**_____

DATE PLANTED:_____ **PRICE:**_____ _____

SUNLIGHT: ☼ ◑ ●
WATER: 💧 💧💧 💧💧💧

○ SEED
○ TRANSPLANT

○ VEGETABLE ○ ORNAMENTAL **PLANT**
○ FRUIT ○ HERB **TYPE**

LIFE CYCLE: ○ ANNUAL ○ BIENNIAL ○ PERENNIAL

SOWN FROM SEED	STARTED TRANSPLANT
SUPPLIER:	SUPPLIER:
COST:	COST:
DATE SOWN:	DATE PLANTED:
DATE GERMINATE:	DATE BLOOMED:
DATE PLANTED OUT:	**RATE IT** ☆☆☆☆☆
DATE BLOOMED:	

DATE	EVENT

OUTCOME	USES

WEATHER LOG
33 ROWS TO LOG IN

Code	Date	Temperature	Humidity	Dew Point	Wind Speed	Wind Direction	Barometric Pressure	Rain Fall	Frost	Snow

General Observation :

Page:

February

MON	TUE	WED	THUR
☐	☐	☐	☐
☐	☐	☐	☐
☐	☐	☐	☐
☐	☐	☐	☐
☐	☐	☐	☐

	FRI	SAT	SUN
☐	☐	☐
☐	☐	☐
☐	☐	☐
☐	☐	☐
☐	☐	☐

KEY DATES

PRIORITY

TO DO LIST

DATE ....

TOP 3 MON THE WED THU FRI SAT SUN

1.

2.

3.

To Do's	Priorities
★	
★	
★	
★	
★	
★	
★	
★	
★	
★	
★	
★	

NOTES

....

....

....

....

....

SOW/TRANSPLANTS

DATE ....

Sow	Transplants
★	★ ....
★	★ ....
★	★ ....
★	★ ....
★	★ ....
★	★ ....
★	★ ....
★	★ ....
★	★ ....
★	★ ....
★	★ ....
★	★ ....
★	★ ....
★	★ ....
★	★ ....
★	★ ....

NOTES

....

....

....

....

SHOPPING LIST

DATE ....   MON THE WED THU FRI SAT SUN

★ ....
★ ....
★ ....
★ ....
★ ....
★ ....
★ ....
★ ....
★ ....
★ ....
★ ....
★ ....
★ ....
★ ....
★ ....
★ ....

★ ....
★ ....
★ ....
★ ....
★ ....
★ ....
★ ....
★ ....
★ ....
★ ....
★ ....
★ ....
★ ....
★ ....
★ ....
★ ....

NOTES

....
....
....
....

Plant Log

PLANT NAME: _____ **PURCHASE AT:** _____

DATE PLANTED: _____ **PRICE:** _____ _____

SUNLIGHT: ☼ ◑ ●
WATER: 💧 💧💧 💧💧💧

○ SEED
○ TRANSPLANT

○ VEGETABLE ○ ORNAMENTAL **PLANT**
○ FRUIT ○ HERB **TYPE**

LIFE CYCLE: ○ ANNUAL ○ BIENNIAL ○ PERENNIAL

SOWN FROM SEED	STARTED TRANSPLANT
SUPPLIER:	SUPPLIER:
COST:	COST:
DATE SOWN:	DATE PLANTED:
DATE GERMINATE:	DATE BLOOMED:
DATE PLANTED OUT:	**RATE IT** ☆ ☆ ☆ ☆ ☆
DATE BLOOMED:	

DATE	EVENT

OUTCOME	USES

WEATHER LOG
33 ROWS TO LOG IN

Code	Date	Temperature	Humidity	Dew Point	Wind Speed	Wind Direction	Barometric Pressure	Rain Fall	Frost	Snow

General Observation :

Page:

MARCH

MON	TUE	WED	THUR
☐	☐	☐	☐
☐	☐	☐	☐
☐	☐	☐	☐
☐	☐	☐	☐
☐	☐	☐	☐

FRI	SAT	SUN
☐	☐	☐
☐	☐	☐
☐	☐	☐
☐	☐	☐
☐	☐	☐

KEY DATES

PRIORITY

TO DO LIST

DATE ....

TOP 3   MON THE WED THU FRI SAT SUN

1.

2.

3.

To Do's	Priorities
★	
★	
★	
★	
★	
★	
★	
★	
★	
★	
★	
★	

NOTES

....

....

....

....

....

SOW/TRANSPLANTS

DATE ....   MON THE WED THU FRI SAT SUN

Sow	Transplants
★	★ ....
★	★ ....
★	★ ....
★	★ ....
★	★ ....
★	★ ....
★	★ ....
★	★ ....
★	★ ....
★	★ ....
★	★ ....
★	★ ....
★	★ ....
★	★ ....
★	★ ....
★	★ ....

NOTES

....
....
....
....

SHOPPING LIST

DATE ....

MON THE WED THU FRI SAT SUN

★ ....

★ ....

★ ....

★ ....

★ ....

★ ....

★ ....

★ ....

★ ....

★ ....

★ ....

★ ....

★ ....

★ ....

★ ....

★ ....

★ ....

★ ....

★ ....

★ ....

★ ....

★ ....

★ ....

★ ....

★ ....

★ ....

★ ....

★ ....

★ ....

★ ....

★ ....

★ ....

NOTES

....

....

....

....

Plant Log

PLANT NAME: _____ **PURCHASE AT:** _____

DATE PLANTED: _____ **PRICE:** _____ _____

SUNLIGHT: ☀ ◐ ●
WATER: 💧 💧 💧

○ SEED
○ TRANSPLANT

○ VEGETABLE ○ ORNAMENTAL **PLANT**
○ FRUIT ○ HERB **TYPE**

LIFE CYCLE: ○ ANNUAL ○ BIENNIAL ○ PERENNIAL

SOWN FROM SEED	STARTED TRANSPLANT
SUPPLIER:	SUPPLIER:
COST:	COST:
DATE SOWN:	DATE PLANTED:
DATE GERMINATE:	DATE BLOOMED:
DATE PLANTED OUT:	**RATE IT** ☆ ☆ ☆ ☆ ☆
DATE BLOOMED:	

DATE	EVENT

OUTCOME	USES

WEATHER LOG
33 ROWS TO LOG IN

Code	Date	Temperature	Humidity	Dew Point	Wind Speed	Wind Direction	Barometric Pressure	Rain Fall	Frost	Snow

General Observation :

APRIL

MON	TUE	WED	THUR
☐	☐	☐	☐
☐	☐	☐	☐
☐	☐	☐	☐
☐	☐	☐	☐
☐	☐	☐	☐

FRI	SAT	SUN
☐	☐	☐
☐	☐	☐
☐	☐	☐
☐	☐	☐
☐	☐	☐

KEY DATES

PRIORITY

TO DO LIST

DATE ....

TOP 3   MON THE WED THU FRI SAT SUN

1.   2.   3.

To Do's	Priorities
★	
★	
★	
★	
★	
★	
★	
★	
★	
★	
★	
★	

NOTES

....
....
....
....
....

SOW/TRANSPLANTS

DATE ....

Sow	Transplants
★	★ ....
★	★ ....
★	★ ....
★	★ ....
★	★ ....
★	★ ....
★	★ ....
★	★ ....
★	★ ....
★	★ ....
★	★ ....
★	★ ....
★	★ ....
★	★ ....
★	★ ....
★	★ ....

NOTES

....

....

....

....

SHOPPING LIST

DATE .... MON THE WED THU FRI SAT SUN

★ ....
★ ....
★ ....
★ ....
★ ....
★ ....
★ ....
★ ....
★ ....
★ ....
★ ....
★ ....
★ ....
★ ....
★ ....
★ ....

★ ....
★ ....
★ ....
★ ....
★ ....
★ ....
★ ....
★ ....
★ ....
★ ....
★ ....
★ ....
★ ....
★ ....
★ ....
★ ....

NOTES

....
....
....
....

Plant Log

PLANT NAME: _____ **PURCHASE AT:** _____

DATE PLANTED: _____ **PRICE:** _____ _____

SUNLIGHT: ☀ ◐ ●
WATER: 💧 💧 💧

○ SEED
○ TRANSPLANT

○ VEGETABLE ○ ORNAMENTAL **PLANT**
○ FRUIT ○ HERB **TYPE**

LIFE CYCLE: ○ ANNUAL ○ BIENNIAL ○ PERENNIAL

SOWN FROM SEED	STARTED TRANSPLANT
SUPPLIER:	SUPPLIER:
COST:	COST:
DATE SOWN:	DATE PLANTED:
DATE GERMINATE:	DATE BLOOMED:
DATE PLANTED OUT:	**RATE IT** ☆ ☆ ☆ ☆ ☆
DATE BLOOMED:	

DATE	EVENT

OUTCOME	USES

WEATHER LOG
33 ROWS TO LOG IN

Code	Date	Temperature	Humidity	Dew Point	Wind Speed	Wind Direction	Barometric Pressure	Rain Fall	Frost	Snow

General Observation :

Page:

MAY

MON	TUE	WED	THUR
☐	☐	☐	☐
☐	☐	☐	☐
☐	☐	☐	☐
☐	☐	☐	☐
☐	☐	☐	☐

FRI	SAT	SUN
☐	☐	☐
☐	☐	☐
☐	☐	☐
☐	☐	☐
☐	☐	☐

KEY DATES

PRIORITY

TO DO LIST

DATE ....

TOP 3   MON THE WED THU FRI SAT SUN

1.   2.   3.

To Do's	Priorities
★ ••	
★ ••	
★ ••	
★ ••	
★ ••	
★ ••	
★ ••	
★ ••	
★ ••	
★ ••	
★ ••	

NOTES

....

....

....

....

....

SOW/TRANSPLANTS

DATE .... MON THE WED THU FRI SAT SUN

Sow	Transplants
★	★ ....
★	★ ....
★	★ ....
★	★ ....
★	★ ....
★	★ ....
★	★ ....
★	★ ....
★	★ ....
★	★ ....
★	★ ....
★	★ ....
★	★ ....
★	★ ....
★	★ ....
★	★ ....

NOTES
....
....
....
....

SHOPPING LIST

DATE ....

MON THE WED THU FRI SAT SUN

★ ....
★ ....
★ ....
★ ....
★ ....
★ ....
★ ....
★ ....
★ ....
★ ....
★ ....
★ ....
★ ....
★ ....
★ ....
★ ....

★ ....
★ ....
★ ....
★ ....
★ ....
★ ....
★ ....
★ ....
★ ....
★ ....
★ ....
★ ....
★ ....
★ ....
★ ....
★ ....

NOTES

....
....
....
....

Plant Log

PLANT NAME: _____ **PURCHASE AT:** _____

DATE PLANTED: _____ **PRICE:** _____ _____

SUNLIGHT: ☀ ◑ ●
WATER: ◊ ◊◊ ◊◊

○ SEED
○ TRANSPLANT

○ VEGETABLE   ○ ORNAMENTAL   **PLANT**
○ FRUIT   ○ HERB   **TYPE**

LIFE CYCLE: ○ ANNUAL   ○ BIENNIAL   ○ PERENNIAL

SOWN FROM SEED	STARTED TRANSPLANT
SUPPLIER:	SUPPLIER:
COST:	COST:
DATE SOWN:	DATE PLANTED:
DATE GERMINATE:	DATE BLOOMED:
DATE PLANTED OUT:	**RATE IT** ☆☆☆☆☆
DATE BLOOMED:	

DATE	EVENT

OUTCOME	USES

WEATHER LOG
33 ROWS TO LOG IN

Code	Date	Temperature	Humidity	Dew Point	Wind Speed	Wind Direction	Barometric Pressure	Rain Fall	Frost	Snow

General Observation :

Page:

JUNE

MON	TUE	WED	THUR
☐	☐	☐	☐
☐	☐	☐	☐
☐	☐	☐	☐
☐	☐	☐	☐
☐	☐	☐	☐

FRI	SAT	SUN
☐	☐	☐
☐	☐	☐
☐	☐	☐
☐	☐	☐
☐	☐	☐

KEY DATES

PRIORITY

SEASONS TO-DO LIST

SPRING

- ○ _____
- ○ _____
- ○ _____
- ○ _____
- ○ _____
- ○ _____
- ○ _____
- ○ _____
- ○ _____
- ○ _____

SUMMER

- ○ _____
- ○ _____
- ○ _____
- ○ _____
- ○ _____
- ○ _____
- ○ _____
- ○ _____
- ○ _____
- ○ _____

FALL

- ○ _____
- ○ _____
- ○ _____
- ○ _____
- ○ _____
- ○ _____
- ○ _____
- ○ _____
- ○ _____
- ○ _____

WINTER

- ○ _____
- ○ _____
- ○ _____
- ○ _____
- ○ _____
- ○ _____
- ○ _____
- ○ _____
- ○ _____
- ○ _____

TO DO LIST

DATE ....

TOP 3　　MON THE WED THU FRI SAT SUN

1.   2.   3.

To Do's	Priorities
★ ··	
★ ··	
★ ··	
★ ··	
★ ··	
★ ··	
★ ··	
★ ··	
★ ··	
★ ··	
★ ··	
★ ··	

NOTES

··

··

··

··

··

SOW/TRANSPLANTS

DATE ....

Sow	Transplants
★...	★...
★...	★...
★...	★...
★...	★...
★...	★...
★...	★...
★...	★...
★...	★...
★...	★...
★...	★...
★...	★...
★...	★...
★...	★...
★...	★...
★...	★...
★...	★...

NOTES

....
....
....
....

SHOPPING LIST

DATE ....

MON THE WED THU FRI SAT SUN

★ ....
★ ....
★ ....
★ ....
★ ....
★ ....
★ ....
★ ....
★ ....
★ ....
★ ....
★ ....
★ ....
★ ....
★ ....
★ ....
★ ....

★ ....
★ ....
★ ....
★ ....
★ ....
★ ....
★ ....
★ ....
★ ....
★ ....
★ ....
★ ....
★ ....
★ ....
★ ....
★ ....
★ ....

NOTES

....
....
....
....

Plant Log

PLANT NAME: _____ **PURCHASE AT:** _____

DATE PLANTED: _____ **PRICE:** _____ _____

SUNLIGHT: **WATER:**

○ SEED
○ TRANSPLANT

○ VEGETABLE   ○ ORNAMENTAL **PLANT**
○ FRUIT   ○ HERB   **TYPE**

LIFE CYCLE: ○ ANNUAL   ○ BIENNIAL   ○ PERENNIAL

SOWN FROM SEED	STARTED TRANSPLANT
SUPPLIER:	SUPPLIER:
COST:	COST:
DATE SOWN:	DATE PLANTED:
DATE GERMINATE:	DATE BLOOMED:
DATE PLANTED OUT:	**RATE IT** ☆ ☆ ☆ ☆ ☆
DATE BLOOMED:	

DATE	EVENT

OUTCOME	USES

WEATHER LOG
33 ROWS TO LOG IN

Code	Date	Temperature	Humidity	Dew Point	Wind Speed	Wind Direction	Barometric Pressure	Rain Fall	Frost	Snow

General Observation :

Page:

July

MON	TUE	WED	THUR
☐	☐	☐	☐
☐	☐	☐	☐
☐	☐	☐	☐
☐	☐	☐	☐
☐	☐	☐	☐

FRI	SAT	SUN
☐	☐	☐
☐	☐	☐
☐	☐	☐
☐	☐	☐
☐	☐	☐

KEY DATES

PRIORITY

TO DO LIST

DATE ....

TOP 3   MON THE WED THU FRI SAT SUN

1.   2.   3.

To Do's	Priorities
★	
★	
★	
★	
★	
★	
★	
★	
★	
★	
★	
★	

NOTES

....

....

....

....

....

SOW/TRANSPLANTS

DATE ....

MON THE WED THU FRI SAT SUN

Sow	Transplants
★	★ ....
★	★ ....
★	★ ....
★	★ ....
★	★ ....
★	★ ....
★	★ ....
★	★ ....
★	★ ....
★	★ ....
★	★ ....
★	★ ....
★	★ ....
★	★ ....
★	★ ....
★	★ ....
★	★ ....

NOTES

....

....

....

....

SHOPPING LIST

DATE ....

MON THE WED THU FRI SAT SUN

★ ....
★ ....
★ ....
★ ....
★ ....
★ ....
★ ....
★ ....
★ ....
★ ....
★ ....
★ ....
★ ....
★ ....
★ ....
★ ....

★ ....
★ ....
★ ....
★ ....
★ ....
★ ....
★ ....
★ ....
★ ....
★ ....
★ ....
★ ....
★ ....
★ ....
★ ....
★ ....

NOTES

....
....
....
....

Plant Log

PLANT NAME:_____ **PURCHASE AT:**_____

DATE PLANTED:_____ **PRICE:**_____ _____

SUNLIGHT: ☀ ◑ ● ○ SEED ○ VEGETABLE ○ ORNAMENTAL **PLANT**
WATER: 💧 💧 💧 ○ TRANSPLANT ○ FRUIT ○ HERB **TYPE**

LIFE CYCLE: ○ ANNUAL ○ BIENNIAL ○ PERENNIAL

SOWN FROM SEED	STARTED TRANSPLANT
SUPPLIER:	SUPPLIER:
COST:	COST:
DATE SOWN:	DATE PLANTED:
DATE GERMINATE:	DATE BLOOMED:
DATE PLANTED OUT:	**RATE IT** ☆ ☆ ☆ ☆ ☆
DATE BLOOMED:	

DATE	EVENT

OUTCOME	USES

WEATHER LOG
33 ROWS TO LOG IN

Code	Date	Temperature	Humidity	Dew Point	Wind Speed	Wind Direction	Barometric Pressure	Rain Fall	Frost	Snow

General Observation :

Page:

August

MON	TUE	WED	THUR
☐	☐	☐	☐
☐	☐	☐	☐
☐	☐	☐	☐
☐	☐	☐	☐
☐	☐	☐	☐

FRI	SAT	SUN
☐	☐	☐
☐	☐	☐
☐	☐	☐
☐	☐	☐
☐	☐	☐

KEY DATES

PRIORITY

TO DO LIST

DATE ....

TOP 3   MON THE WED THU FRI SAT SUN

1.

2.

3.

To Do's	Priorities
★	
★	
★	
★	
★	
★	
★	
★	
★	
★	
★	

NOTES

....

....

....

....

....

SOW/TRANSPLANTS

DATE ....   MON THE WED THU FRI SAT SUN

Sow	Transplants
★	★ ....
★	★ ....
★	★ ....
★	★ ....
★	★ ....
★	★ ....
★	★ ....
★	★ ....
★	★ ....
★	★ ....
★	★ ....
★	★ ....
★	★ ....
★	★ ....
★	★ ....
★	★ ....

NOTES

....

....

....

....

SHOPPING LIST

MON THE WED THU FRI SAT SUN

★ ....

★ ....

★ ....

★ ....

★ ....

★ ....

★ ....

★ ....

★ ....

★ ....

★ ....

★ ....

★ ....

★ ....

★ ....

★ ....

★ ....

★ ....

★ ....

★ ....

★ ....

★ ....

★ ....

★ ....

★ ....

★ ....

★ ....

★ ....

★ ....

★ ....

★ ....

★ ....

NOTES

....

....

....

....

Plant Log

PLANT NAME:_____   **PURCHASE AT:**_____

DATE PLANTED:_____   **PRICE:**_____

SUNLIGHT: ☀ ◑ ⬤   ○ SEED   ○ VEGETABLE   ○ ORNAMENTAL   **PLANT**
WATER: 💧 💧 💧   ○ TRANSPLANT   ○ FRUIT   ○ HERB   **TYPE**

LIFE CYCLE: ○ ANNUAL   ○ BIENNIAL   ○ PERENNIAL

SOWN FROM SEED	STARTED TRANSPLANT
SUPPLIER:	SUPPLIER:
COST:	COST:
DATE SOWN:	DATE PLANTED:
DATE GERMINATE:	DATE BLOOMED:
DATE PLANTED OUT:	**RATE IT** ☆ ☆ ☆ ☆ ☆
DATE BLOOMED:	

DATE	EVENT

OUTCOME	USES

WEATHER LOG
33 ROWS TO LOG IN

Code	Date	Temperature	Humidity	Dew Point	Wind Speed	Wind Direction	Barometric Pressure	Rain Fall	Frost	Snow

General Observation :

Page:

September

MON	TUE	WED	THUR
☐	☐	☐	☐
☐	☐	☐	☐
☐	☐	☐	☐
☐	☐	☐	☐
☐	☐	☐	☐

FRI	SAT	SUN
☐	☐	☐
☐	☐	☐
☐	☐	☐
☐	☐	☐
☐	☐	☐

KEY DATES

PRIORITY

TO DO LIST

DATE ....

TOP 3 MON THE WED THU FRI SAT SUN

1. 2. 3.

To Do's	Priorities
★	
★	
★	
★	
★	
★	
★	
★	
★	
★	
★	
★	

NOTES

....

....

....

....

....

SOW/TRANSPLANTS

DATE ....

Sow	Transplants
★	★ ....
★	★ ....
★	★ ....
★	★ ....
★	★ ....
★	★ ....
★	★ ....
★	★ ....
★	★ ....
★	★ ....
★	★ ....
★	★ ....
★	★ ....
★	★ ....
★	★ ....
★	★ ....

NOTES

....

....

....

....

SHOPPING LIST

DATE ....

MON THE WED THU FRI SAT SUN

- ★ ....
- ★ ....
- ★ ....
- ★ ....
- ★ ....
- ★ ....
- ★ ....
- ★ ....
- ★ ....
- ★ ....
- ★ ....
- ★ ....
- ★ ....
- ★ ....
- ★ ....
- ★ ....

- ★ ....
- ★ ....
- ★ ....
- ★ ....
- ★ ....
- ★ ....
- ★ ....
- ★ ....
- ★ ....
- ★ ....
- ★ ....
- ★ ....
- ★ ....
- ★ ....
- ★ ....
- ★ ....

NOTES

....

....

....

....

Plant Log

PLANT NAME:_____ **PURCHASE AT:**_____

DATE PLANTED:_____ **PRICE:**_____ _____

SUNLIGHT: ☀ ◑ ●
WATER: 💧 💧💧 💧💧💧

○ SEED
○ TRANSPLANT

○ VEGETABLE ○ ORNAMENTAL **PLANT**
○ FRUIT ○ HERB **TYPE**

LIFE CYCLE: ○ ANNUAL ○ BIENNIAL ○ PERENNIAL

SOWN FROM SEED	STARTED TRANSPLANT
SUPPLIER:	SUPPLIER:
COST:	COST:
DATE SOWN:	DATE PLANTED:
DATE GERMINATE:	DATE BLOOMED:
DATE PLANTED OUT:	**RATE IT** ☆ ☆ ☆ ☆ ☆
DATE BLOOMED:	

DATE	EVENT

OUTCOME	USES

WEATHER LOG
33 ROWS TO LOG IN

Code	Date	Temperature	Humidity	Dew Point	Wind Speed	Wind Direction	Barometric Pressure	Rain Fall	Frost	Snow

General Observation :

Page:

October

MON	TUE	WED	THUR
☐	☐	☐	☐
☐	☐	☐	☐
☐	☐	☐	☐
☐	☐	☐	☐
☐	☐	☐	☐

FRI	SAT	SUN
☐	☐	☐
☐	☐	☐
☐	☐	☐
☐	☐	☐
☐	☐	☐

KEY DATES

PRIORITY

TO DO LIST

DATE ....

TOP 3   MON THE WED THU FRI SAT SUN

1.   2.   3.

To Do's	Priorities
★	
★	
★	
★	
★	
★	
★	
★	
★	
★	
★	
★	

NOTES

....
....
....
....
....

SOW/TRANSPLANTS

DATE ....

Sow	Transplants
★	★ ....
★	★ ....
★	★ ....
★	★ ....
★	★ ....
★	★ ....
★	★ ....
★	★ ....
★	★ ....
★	★ ....
★	★ ....
★	★ ....
★	★ ....
★	★ ....
★	★ ....
★	★ ....

NOTES

....

....

....

....

SHOPPING LIST

DATE .... MON THE WED THU FRI SAT SUN

★ ....
★ ....
★ ....
★ ....
★ ....
★ ....
★ ....
★ ....
★ ....
★ ....
★ ....
★ ....
★ ....
★ ....
★ ....
★ ....

★ ....
★ ....
★ ....
★ ....
★ ....
★ ....
★ ....
★ ....
★ ....
★ ....
★ ....
★ ....
★ ....
★ ....
★ ....
★ ....

NOTES

....

....

....

....

Plant Log

PLANT NAME:_____   **PURCHASE AT:**_____

DATE PLANTED:_____   **PRICE:**_____   _____

SUNLIGHT: ☼ ◑ ●
WATER: 💧 💧💧 💧💧

○ SEED
○ TRANSPLANT

○ VEGETABLE   ○ ORNAMENTAL   **PLANT**
○ FRUIT   ○ HERB   **TYPE**

LIFE CYCLE: ○ ANNUAL   ○ BIENNIAL   ○ PERENNIAL

SOWN FROM SEED	STARTED TRANSPLANT
SUPPLIER:	SUPPLIER:
COST:	COST:
DATE SOWN:	DATE PLANTED:
DATE GERMINATE:	DATE BLOOMED:
DATE PLANTED OUT:	**RATE IT** ☆☆☆☆☆
DATE BLOOMED:	

DATE	EVENT

OUTCOME	USES

WEATHER LOG
33 ROWS TO LOG IN

Code	Date	Temperature	Humidity	Dew Point	Wind Speed	Wind Direction	Barometric Pressure	Rain Fall	Frost	Snow

General Observation :

Page:

November

MON	TUE	WED	THUR
☐	☐	☐	☐
☐	☐	☐	☐
☐	☐	☐	☐
☐	☐	☐	☐
☐	☐	☐	☐

FRI	SAT	SUN
☐	☐	☐
☐	☐	☐
☐	☐	☐
☐	☐	☐
☐	☐	☐

KEY DATES

PRIORITY

TO DO LIST

DATE ....

TOP 3   MON THE WED THU FRI SAT SUN

1.   2.   3.

To Do's	Priorities
★	
★	
★	
★	
★	
★	
★	
★	
★	
★	
★	

NOTES

....

....

....

....

....

SOW/TRANSPLANTS

DATE ....

Sow	Transplants
★	★ ....
★	★ ....
★	★ ....
★	★ ....
★	★ ....
★	★ ....
★	★ ....
★	★ ....
★	★ ....
★	★ ....
★	★ ....
★	★ ....
★	★ ....
★	★ ....
★	★ ....
★	★ ....

NOTES

....

....

....

....

SHOPPING LIST

MON THE WED THU FRI SAT SUN

- ★ ....
- ★ ....
- ★ ....
- ★ ....
- ★ ....
- ★ ....
- ★ ....
- ★ ....
- ★ ....
- ★ ....
- ★ ....
- ★ ....
- ★ ....
- ★ ....
- ★ ....
- ★ ....

- ★ ....
- ★ ....
- ★ ....
- ★ ....
- ★ ....
- ★ ....
- ★ ....
- ★ ....
- ★ ....
- ★ ....
- ★ ....
- ★ ....
- ★ ....
- ★ ....
- ★ ....

NOTES

....

....

....

....

Plant Log

PLANT NAME:_____ **PURCHASE AT:**_____

DATE PLANTED:_____ **PRICE:**_____ _____

SUNLIGHT: ☀ ◑ ●
WATER: 💧 💧💧 💧💧💧

○ SEED
○ TRANSPLANT

○ VEGETABLE ○ ORNAMENTAL **PLANT**
○ FRUIT ○ HERB **TYPE**

LIFE CYCLE: ○ ANNUAL ○ BIENNIAL ○ PERENNIAL

SOWN FROM SEED	STARTED TRANSPLANT
SUPPLIER:	SUPPLIER:
COST:	COST:
DATE SOWN:	DATE PLANTED:
DATE GERMINATE:	DATE BLOOMED:
DATE PLANTED OUT:	**RATE IT** ☆☆☆☆☆
DATE BLOOMED:	

DATE	EVENT

OUTCOME	USES

WEATHER LOG
33 ROWS TO LOG IN

Code	Date	Temperature	Humidity	Dew Point	Wind Speed	Wind Direction	Barometric Pressure	Rain Fall	Frost	Snow

General Observation :

Page:

December

MON	TUE	WED	THUR
☐	☐	☐	☐
☐	☐	☐	☐
☐	☐	☐	☐
☐	☐	☐	☐
☐	☐	☐	☐

FRI	SAT	SUN
☐	☐	☐
☐	☐	☐
☐	☐	☐
☐	☐	☐
☐	☐	☐

KEY DATES

PRIORITY

TO DO LIST

DATE ....

TOP 3   MON THE WED THU FRI SAT SUN

1.   2.   3.

To Do's	Priorities
★ ··	
★ ··	
★ ··	
★ ··	
★ ··	
★ ··	
★ ··	
★ ··	
★ ··	
★ ··	
★ ··	
★ ··	

NOTES

··
··
··
··
··

SOW/TRANSPLANTS

DATE ....

Sow	Transplants
★	★ ....
★	★ ....
★	★ ....
★	★ ....
★	★ ....
★	★ ....
★	★ ....
★	★ ....
★	★ ....
★	★ ....
★	★ ....
★	★ ....
★	★ ....
★	★ ....
★	★ ....
★	★ ....

NOTES

....

....

....

....

SHOPPING LIST

★	★ ....
★	★ ....
★	★ ....
★	★ ....
★	★ ....
★	★ ....
★	★ ....
★	★ ....
★	★ ....
★	★ ....
★	★ ....
★	★ ....
★	★ ....
★	★ ....
★	★ ....
★	★ ....
★	★ ....

NOTES

....

....

....

....

Plant Log

PLANT NAME:_____   **PURCHASE AT:**_____

DATE PLANTED:_____   **PRICE:**_____   _____

SUNLIGHT: ☼ ◑ ●
WATER: 💧 💧💧 💧

○ SEED
○ TRANSPLANT

○ VEGETABLE   ○ ORNAMENTAL   **PLANT**
○ FRUIT   ○ HERB   **TYPE**

LIFE CYCLE: ○ ANNUAL   ○ BIENNIAL   ○ PERENNIAL

SOWN FROM SEED	STARTED TRANSPLANT
SUPPLIER:	SUPPLIER:
COST:	COST:
DATE SOWN:	DATE PLANTED:
DATE GERMINATE:	DATE BLOOMED:
DATE PLANTED OUT:	**RATE IT** ☆☆☆☆☆
DATE BLOOMED:	

DATE	EVENT

OUTCOME	USES

WEATHER LOG
33 ROWS TO LOG IN

Code	Date	Temperature	Humidity	Dew Point	Wind Speed	Wind Direction	Barometric Pressure	Rain Fall	Frost	Snow

General Observation :

Page:

YOUR GARDEN JOURNAL
DATE

YOUR BEST PICTURE

_____

_____

_____

_____

_____

_____

_____

_____

_____

_____

_____

_____

YOUR BEST PICTURE

YOUR GARDEN JOURNAL
DATE

_____

_____

_____

_____

_____

_____

_____

_____

_____

_____

_____

_____

YOUR BEST PICTURE

YOUR BEST PICTURE

YOUR BEST PICTURE

YOUR GARDEN JOURNAL
DATE _____

BLANK SCHEDULERS

BLANK SCHEDULERS

◯ Maintenance   ◯ Blooming, Fruit & Harvest   ◯   ◯
◯ Planting   ◯ Garden Activity   ◯   ◯

BLANK SCHEDULERS

BLANK SCHEDULERS

WEATHER LOG
33 ROWS TO LOG IN

Code	Date	Temperature	Humidity	Dew Point	Wind Speed	Wind Direction	Barometric Pressure	Rain Fall	Frost	Snow

General Observation :

Page:

WEATHER LOG
33 ROWS TO LOG IN

Code	Date	Temperature	Humidity	Dew Point	Wind Speed	Wind Direction	Barometric Pressure	Rain Fall	Frost	Snow

General Observation :   Page:

Pest And Diseases Treatment Log

Code	Date	Plant	Sysmptom	Treatment	Reapplied	Results

Notes

_____

_____

_____

_____

_____

_____

_____

Pest And Diseases Treatment Log

Code	Date	Plant	Sysmptom	Treatment	Reapplied	Results

Notes

Pest And Diseases Treatment Log

Code	Date	Plant	Sysmptom	Treatment	Reapplied	Results

Notes

_____
_____
_____
_____
_____
_____
_____
_____

Pest And Diseases Treatment Log

Code	Date	Plant	Sysmptom	Treatment	Reapplied	Results

Notes

Pest And Diseases Treatment Log

Code	Date	Plant	Sysmptom	Treatment	Reapplied	Results

Notes

_____

_____

_____

_____

_____

_____

_____

_____

Sketch

Sketch

Sketch

Sketch

Made in the USA
Middletown, DE
08 January 2023

21676288R00071